# THE SECRET WORLD OF

# Frogs and Toads

# THE SECRET WORLD OF

# Frogs and Toads

**Jill Bailey**

Chicago, Illinois

Project Editors: Geoff Barker, Marta Segal Block, Sarah Jameson, Jennifer Mattson
Production Manager: Brian Suderski
Consultants: Michael Chinery and Dr. Eric L. Peters
Illustrated by Stuart Lafford, Colin Newman, and Richard Orr
Designed by Ian Winton
Picture research by Vashti Gwynn
Planned and produced by Discovery Books
Printed and bound in the United States by Lake Book Manufacturing, Inc.
07 06 05 04 03
10 9 8 7 6 5 4 3 2 1

**Library of Congress Cataloging-in-Publication Data**
Bailey, Jill.
  Frogs and toads / Jill Bailey.
     v. cm. -- (The secret world of)
Includes bibliographical references (p.   ).
Contents: Where frogs and toads live -- Food and feeding -- Reproduction
-- Changing shape -- Swimming and jumping -- Frog senses -- Frog
defenses -- Frogs in danger.
  ISBN 0-7398-7022-X (lib. bdg. : hardcover)
  1.  Anura--Juvenile literature. [1. Frogs. 2. Toads.]  I. Title. II.
Series.
  QL668.E2B277 2003
  597.8--dc21

                    2003002151

**Acknowledgments**
The publishers would like to thank the following for permission to reproduce photographs:
*p.8 Mike Linley/SAL/Oxford Scientific Films; p.9 Mark Bowler/Natural History Photographic Agency; pp.10, 22, 25, 26, 29, 30, 39, 42 Michael Fogden/Oxford Scientific Films; p.11 T. Kitchin & V. Hurst/Natural History Photographic Agency; p.12, 18 Jane Burton/Bruce Coleman Collection; p.13 Anthony Bannister/Natural History Photographic Agency; p.14, 16, 35 Zig Leszczynski/Animals Animals/Oxford Scientific Films; p.15 Ant Photo Library/Natural History Photographic Agency; p.17 Paulo De Oliveira/Oxford Scientific Films; p.19 Paulo De Oliveira/Oxford Scientific Films; p.20 Michael Durham/ www.durmphoto.com; p.21 Yves Lanceau/Natural History Photographic Agency;  p.23 E.A. Janes/Natural History Photographic Agency; p.24 M.P.L. Fogden/Bruce Coleman Collection; p.27 Kim Taylor/Bruce Coleman Collection; p.31 Rodger Jackman/ Oxford Scientific Films; p.33 Stephen Dalton/Natural History Photographic Agency; p.34 Michael Sewell/Oxford Scientific Films; p.36 Ken Preston Mafham/Premaphotos Wildlife; p.37 Martin Harvey/Natural History Photographic Agency; p.38 Rod Williams/Bruce Coleman Collection; p.40 Paulo De Oliveira/Oxford Scientific Films; p.41 Juan M. Renjifo/Animals Animals/ Oxford Scientific Films; p.43 W. Perry Conway/Corbis.*

**Other Acknowledgments**
*Cover photo: John Netherton/Oxford Scientific Films*

**Disclaimer**
Every effort has been made to contact copyright holders of any material reproduced in this book. Any omissions will be rectified in subsequent printings if notice is given to the publisher.

**Note to the Reader**
Some words are shown in bold, **like this.** You can find out
what they mean by looking in the glossary.

# Contents

# CHAPTER 1
# Living a Double Life

**Prehistoric amphibians, the ancestors of frogs and toads, were the largest animals on land 300 million years ago. They grew to almost 13 ft (4 m) in length.**

**A group of frogs is called an army. A group of toads is called a knot.**

**The oldest known frog fossil is called *Prosalirus bitis,* a name that comes from the Latin word *prosalire* ("to leap forward") and the Navajo word *bitis* ("high over it"). It lived during the Jurassic Period, about 190 million years ago, in what is now Arizona.**

**The largest anuran in the world is the Goliath frog from West Africa. Its head and body length is over 1 ft (30 cm).**

**At less than 0.5 in. (1 cm) long, the Cuban tree frog is the world's smallest frog.**

Frogs and toads are small, four-legged animals with webbed hind feet, large bulging eyes, a wide mouth and soft, somewhat slimy skin. Their hind legs are much longer and stronger than their front legs, and are used for jumping and swimming.

There are about 4,700 different kinds, or **species,** of frogs and toads. They belong to a group of **vertebrates** (animals with backbones) called **amphibians,** which are animals that live both on land and in water. The young of most frogs and toads are fishlike tadpoles that live in water. They develop into adult frogs and toads, which usually spend at least part of their lives on land.

There are three groups of living amphibians. Salamanders and legless, wormlike animals called caecilians form two of these groups. Frogs and toads belong to the largest group, called **anurans,** from their Latin name *Anura,* which means "without a tail."

▶ Frogs and toads have long hind legs for leaping, webbed feet for swimming, and a large head with bulging eyes. Leopard frogs like this one live in North America.

## FROG OR TOAD?

Frogs and toads are closely related, but there are distinct differences between them. Species with smooth, moist skins and long legs are commonly called frogs, while those with drier, warty skins and shorter legs are usually called toads. Most, but not all, toads tend to walk rather than jump when catching **prey,** but can leap to escape danger.

**Hind legs**
The hind legs are long for jumping and swimming. The hind feet are large and webbed to push against the water.

**Poison glands**
The skin of frogs and toads is covered with glands that produce poisonous **mucus.** Some species have large poison glands on their necks.

**Skin**
Moist skin allows oxygen to pass into the tissues below. It may be brightly colored and patterned.

**Front legs**
The front legs are short and sturdy for landing on after jumping. They are also used to push food down the throat.

**Ears**
The ears do not stick out, but the round eardrums can usually be seen just behind the eyes.

**Head**
Frogs and toads have large, broad heads.

**Mouth**
The mouth opens very wide for grabbing animal prey. Most frogs and toads have a long, sticky tongue.

**Eyes**
Most frogs and toads see well in the dark. Their eyes are very large and bulging, allowing them to see in almost all directions at once.

## MANY KINDS

Frogs and toads come in an astonishing range of colors, shapes, and sizes, from the clawed toads of Africa with their flat, brownish-green bodies, to the brilliantly colored arrow-poison frogs of Central and South America.

All frogs and toads are **ectothermic** (cold-blooded), meaning that they cannot warm themselves up, and their bodies stay roughly the same temperature as their surroundings. For this reason, frogs and toads living in areas that get very cold become completely inactive **(dormant)** during the winter, resuming activity in the spring.

Insects and other small animals, like slugs and worms, form the diet of most frogs and toads. Larger ones may eat other frogs and toads, and even animals as big as mice!

Tropical forests are moist and humid all day, but in many other parts of the world, frogs have to avoid the drying heat of the sun by being **nocturnal.** This means they are active mainly at night and rest during the day.

This Colorado River toad has the fat body, stout, short legs, and warty skin typical of toads. The large, swollen gland behind its round eardrum produces poison to fend off its enemies.

## BREATHING

Adult frogs and toads have lungs and breathe air. By raising the floor of the mouth, they swallow air and force it into the lungs, which take up oxygen and release carbon dioxide. Their hearts pump blood to small vessels under the skin, which also take up oxygen and release carbon dioxide. Before their lungs develop, tadpoles use organs called **gills** to absorb oxygen. Tiny blood vessels carry it throughout the tadpole's body.

# Slimy Skin

The skin of adult frogs and toads is kept moist by a coating of slimy **mucus,** which is made by special glands. The mucus is helpful for climbing because it is sticky. Many frogs and toads also produce chemicals that make their bodies taste bad to other animals, and often these chemicals are poisonous.

Frogs and toads **molt,** or shed their skins regularly, to reveal new ones underneath. The skin splits and the frog uses its front feet to pull the loose skin into its mouth. It then eats it so none of the nutrients go to waste. This red-eyed frog is yawning widely to help remove its old skin.

# CHAPTER 2
# Where Frogs and Toads Live

Frogs and toads must keep their skins moist, so most live in damp places. Swamps, marshes, and pond edges are ideal **habitats.** Most **species** live in the world's warm, moist tropical rain forests. However, frogs and toads can also be found in deserts, on mountains, and in most other parts of the world. In fact, frog fossils have been found on all continents, including Antarctica. Frogs and

This pygmy **marsupial** frog has found a very useful pool inside a bromeliad plant. Her tadpoles will drop into the tiny pool from a pouch on her back.

New species of frog are being identified all the time in remote tropical regions. In fact, in 2002 about 100 new species were discovered in Sri Lanka.

In a just a few acres of South American rain forest there may be more than 80 different species of frog and toad.

The Australian humming frog can dig down in the desert earth to a depth of 4 ft (1.2 m).

A Couch's spadefoot toad can survive for over two years without rain in parts of the Colorado desert.

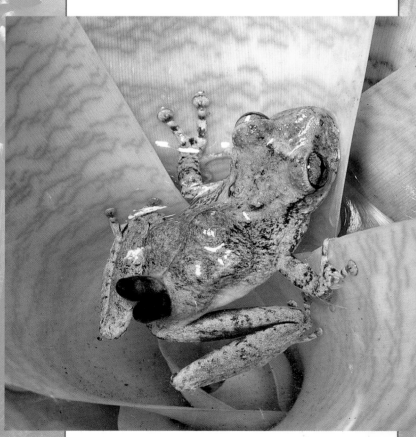

toads no longer live in Antarctica,
but they can be found on every
other continent and on many
ocean islands. The only places they
cannot live are where the ground is
permanently frozen or covered
with ice.

## FROGS OF THE FOREST

In tropical forest habitats, as
elsewhere, frogs are usually most
active at night, when there are
fewer **predators,** such as birds,
to see and catch them. Tree frogs
live high above the ground in the
leaves and branches of forest trees.
Many have skins that are colored,
or **camouflaged,** to match the
colors of leaves or tree trunks.

Some small frogs make use of
pools of water that collect in plants
like bromeliads, which grow high

This red-eyed tree frog has special suckerlike
pads on its feet that help it cling to leaves
and branches. The long, slender legs of tree
frogs are ideal for their acrobatic lifestyle.

on tree branches in rain forests.
These pools can safely hold the
eggs of a frog, and then provide
a tiny pond for the tadpoles once
they have hatched. Other frogs live
on the forest floor, and take shelter
under leaves and logs. Puddles on
the ground offer plenty of places
to lay their eggs.

Tree frogs are excellent climbers.
They walk or climb easily along
branches, jumping only to escape
predators or to leap from tree to
tree. They have slender, somewhat
flat bodies and long limbs. Their
large, bulging eyes help them spot
predators by enabling them to see
in almost all directions at once.

## Aquatic Frogs and Toads

Some frogs and toads are **aquatic,** spending almost all of their lives in water, even as adults. The African clawed toad and the South American Surinam toad have very flattened bodies. All four of their feet are webbed. These toads live near the bottom of lakes and ponds, where they feed on small fish, worms, and aquatic insects. Their eyes are almost on the tops of their heads, rather than at the sides. From time to time these aquatic toads swim up to the surface to take a gulp of air into their lungs. They also absorb some oxygen through their skins.

The Lake Titicaca frog lives in the high mountain lakes of the Andes in South America, where the air is thin and oxygen is in short supply. Its skin is very wrinkled and baggy, giving the frog more skin through which to absorb oxygen.

Many frogs that live in fast-flowing rivers and waterfalls have large suction pads on their front and back feet to help them cling to wet rocks. For the same reason, their tadpoles often have suckerlike mouths, and often a second sucker on the belly, too.

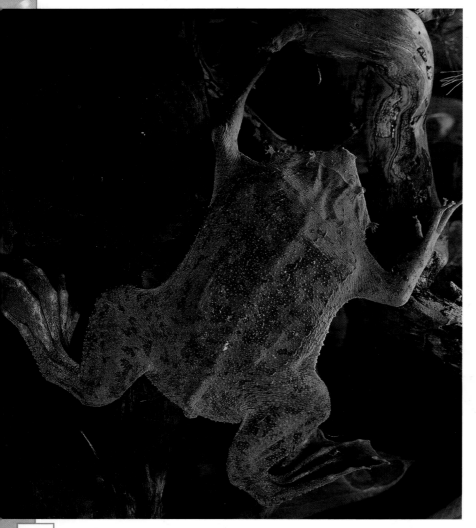

The Surinam toad spends its whole life underwater and has huge, webbed hind feet.

## KEEPING WARM

Although warm, wet places are ideal for frogs, some have **evolved** special **adaptations** that allow them to survive in unusually cold or dry areas.

For example, Atelopus toads live in large numbers in the chilly streams of the Andes mountains. Because they are fatter than their tropical relatives, they are well **insulated** against the cold so that they lose less heat from their bodies. Their skin is very dark, too, which helps them stay warm because darker colors absorb more heat than lighter ones. They are also **diurnal**

A dormant African bullfrog peers sleepily out of its burrow. The photographer has made a hole in the burrow to find the frog.

(active during the day) because it is warmer when the sun is out.

In colder climates, frogs and toads are often active only at warmer times of the year and become **dormant** during the winter. They find a sheltered place, such as a **burrow,** a den under a log or stone, or sometimes a tool shed or a garage. Their breathing and other body processes slow down, so they use little energy. If they have fed well enough in the fall, they can live on their fat until springtime.

## NATURAL ANTIFREEZE

During **dormancy** frogs and toads in cold areas are able to survive icy temperatures without freezing solid. Many toads simply **burrow** into the ground to protect themselves from the cold. Frogs, which are less suited to burrowing than toads, avoid freezing in another way. Their body cells produce special substances that lower the point at which liquid freezes. This keeps frogs' cells from freezing and possibly bursting. It works much like the antifreeze that humans add to their car engines during cold winter months.

## SURVIVAL ON LAND

Some frogs and toads live mostly on land, even in hot, dry deserts. They do not drink, but soak in water through their absorbent skin. In very dry climates, they are in danger of drying out and dying.

Land-dwelling frogs and toads have thicker skins than **aquatic** frogs. This helps prevent water from leaving their bodies through their skin. But if they do lose a lot of water, their bodies are like dry

Spadefoot toads have developed spadelike structures on their hind feet for digging.

sponges—as soon as conditions become wet again, they can very quickly reabsorb the moisture they need.

When exposed to the sun, the African gray tree frog changes its dark brown or gray skin to white, which reflects the light so the frog does not heat up so quickly. This frog and some others produce a waxy substance that they wipe over their bodies with their legs to help stop water loss. They look as if they are coated in plastic. Some desert frogs save water by **excreting** white crystals of waste (like birds do) instead of liquid urine. They may also go into a sleep called **estivation** during the hottest months.

# Living Sponge

When estivating, the Australian water-holding frog forms a hard cocoon around itself to prevent water loss from its skin. Inside this cocoon is a very fat frog, probably holding more than half of its body weight as water in its bladder. Aboriginal Australian people catch these frogs in the dry season and drink the water.

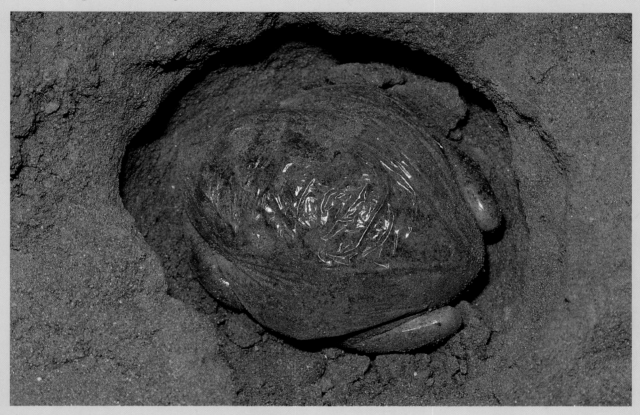

## DIGGING DEEP

The best place to avoid the heat of the sun in the desert is underground. Desert frogs and toads make burrows, and each **species** has developed its own special way of digging. While many spadefoot toads burrow in backward with spadelike feet, the Australian turtle frog and sandhill frog dig in headfirst using their front feet. African shovel-nosed frogs have shovel-shaped snouts protected by hard pads, which they use for burrowing into the ground.

# CHAPTER 3
# Food and Feeding

To swallow food, frogs and toads close their eyes and squeeze their eyeballs down to press on the roof of the mouth. This forces the food down their throats.

When a frog or toad eats something that tastes bad or is poisonous, it can turn its stomach inside out through its mouth and wipe it clean.

At Pretoria Zoo in South Africa, an African bullfrog once ate seventeen young cobra snakes at a single mealtime.

Isecksohn's Brazilian tree frog is one of the few truly vegetarian frogs. It feeds only on fruit. The seeds pass out with its droppings, which helps the plants to spread.

Adult frogs and toads are usually **carnivores** (meat-eaters). Most of them hunt and eat ants, beetles, flies, worms, and slugs. Some tackle **prey** as large as mice, baby birds, and snakes—and other frogs and toads. The American bullfrog eats birds, turtles, fish, and bats, and will sometimes even eat its own young. Giant toads will eat plants and the remains of dead animals. They have even been known to eat dog food!

Generally, frogs and toads are not picky eaters, but there are a few **species** that only like certain foods. The Mexican **burrowing** toad, for example, is very fond of

An American bullfrog uses its front feet to guide a ribbon snake into its mouth.

termites and will lick them up like an anteater. The European common frog prefers snails to insects, and many **aquatic** frogs and toads eat underwater insects or fish.

Most frogs and toads live and hunt on land, preferring to **ambush** their prey than to run after it. Some try to lure prey closer by twitching their toes to mimic worms. In towns and cities, toads may sit under streetlamps at night, feasting on insects attracted to the light. Each toad usually returns to the same lamp.

Frogs and toads have very good vision, but they recognize prey by its movement. If the prey stops moving they will soon lose interest. Bees, wasps, and poisonous or bad-

This toad uses its sticky tongue to pull a centipede into its mouth. By closing its eyes and pushing its eyeballs down into its mouth, the toad forces the prey down its throat.

tasting prey are generally avoided. These often have obvious bands of bright colors that make them easy to recognize.

The simple peglike teeth of frogs and toads are only strong enough to hold small prey. Most have teeth only in the upper jaw, and the jaw itself has notches or sawlike edges. Some also have teeth in the roof of the mouth. Because their teeth are not sharp enough for cutting, frogs and toads swallow their prey whole without chewing. Many toads, and some frogs, have no teeth at all and push food down their throats with their front feet.

## TADPOLE TASTES

Unlike their parents, most tadpoles are **herbivores,** feeding on plants and tiny **algae** that grow underwater. The tadpoles of the Mexican **burrowing** toad and clawed toad trap food particles by pumping water through the mouth and across a special filter of sticky cells.

Most other tadpoles scrape food such as algae from plant and rock surfaces using horny scrapers around their mouths. Sometimes they use their jaws to cut off pieces of soft, rotting plants. The tadpole of the horned toad feeds at the water surface using a mouth that is on the top of its head. Plant-eating tadpoles have very long **intestines,** since plants take a lot of digesting. You can often see the coiled intestine inside a tadpole, because its body wall is almost completely transparent.

Not all tadpoles are herbivores. Some feed on tiny water animals, while others, such as tree frog tadpoles, living in tiny pools of water in bromeliad plants, eat frogs' eggs—often those of their own **species.** In fact, in some

Nothing in nature is wasted. Tadpoles of the European common toad feed on the skin that an adult toad has shed.

arrow-poison frogs, the female actually lays special "food eggs" for her tadpoles to eat.

The tadpoles of some frogs and toads do not have to look for food at all. Instead, they remain inside the eggs, absorbing the yolk until they change into adults. They then hatch as froglets (tiny frogs). This allows the tadpoles to develop in small puddles of water where there is little available food—but also very few **predators.**

# Tongue Tricks

Frogs and toads have a secret weapon: their tongues. In many species the tongue is long and sticky. Attached to the front of the mouth, the tongue is folded back when not in use, but it can be flicked out at lightning speed when an insect comes within range. The tongue sticks to the **prey,** then pulls it back into the frog's mouth. This frog has leaped too late to catch a butterfly for its dinner.

# CHAPTER 4
# Reproduction

Frogs and toads live on their own for most of the year, but come together to breed.

Frogs that live in tropical rain forests may breed almost all year round. Elsewhere, most frogs and toads breed only when there is plenty of water available for their tadpoles to live in. In North America and Europe, for instance, most breed in early springtime. European frogs living near the Arctic Circle mate and lay their eggs while lakes and ponds are still covered in ice.

Many frogs and toads live near water all the time, but others migrate to favorite ponds or lakes to breed.

**To be sure of finding a mate, a male frog or toad will often grab a female long before it is time to breed. He may need to cling on to her for days—or even weeks!**

**When courting, toads such as the yellow-bellied toad from Central Europe call 80 times a minute or more.**

**Fully inflated, the vocal sac of a courting European tree frog is as big as the rest of the frog.**

**The tiny Cuban tree frog lays just a single egg, while large toads such as the giant toad may lay up to 30,000.**

▶ Many female frogs and toads are larger than the males of the same species. This is a pair of tomato frogs. The female on the right is much bigger and more colorful than her mate. Only a few species show this dramatic a difference in color between males and females.

In desert environments, the mating behavior of **species** such as spadefoot toads is triggered by the sound of rain falling. All the toads in the area come out from their underground **burrows** at the same time and lay their eggs on the same night. Their tadpoles develop in just ten days because they need to become frogs quickly before their temporary pool dries up.

### Frogs' Chorus

Most frogs and toads mate at night and females are attracted to males by their calls. Each species has its own pattern of calling. The female's ears are tuned to the particular pitch of calls from her own kind, and she can pick these out, even in the deafening racket of a frogs' chorus made up of several different species. The sound of a male's call, which he makes by inflating his **vocal sac** or sacs, tells a female how big and healthy he is: the louder and deeper the call, the better.

Some closely related species differ only in their calls, but cannot breed together because females of one species do not recognize the calls of the other.

Female frogs are gathering in this pool to breed, attracted there by the loud calls of many male frogs.

Males with soft voices do not always lose out in a loud frogs' chorus. Some natterjack toads stay close to a male with a loud voice in hopes that females will not be able to tell which one is making the more impressive calls.

21

This is not a friendly hug, but a wrestling match. Two male arrow-poison frogs battle over an area of forest in which to hunt.

The calls of a male warn other males to keep out of his area. If calling does not stop an intruder, some frogs try more forceful methods. For example, arrow-poison frogs stand up on their hind legs and wrestle, while other species may bite or stab at rivals. The male Australian tusked frog has tusks in its lower jaw, and some tree frogs have spines on their front legs that can cause fatal injuries.

## READY FOR BATTLE

Some **species** of frogs and toads defend their breeding area from other frogs and toads. In many species, males and females look very similar, although the female is often larger than the male. But in species where males fight over females, the male may be larger in size and sometimes is armed with spines or tusks.

The male South American smith frog encloses his territory in mud walls up to 4 inches (10 centimeters) high. Rainwater collects inside the fenced area, which may be up to 12 inches (30 centimeters) across. He sits in his private pool and calls to attract potential mates.

## GETTING TOGETHER

During the breeding season, the males of many species develop special pads on their feet. The pads have rough surfaces that help the male grip the female, usually behind her front legs. The male clings to the female as she swims around looking for a suitable place to **spawn,** or lay her eggs (which are also called spawn). Species that spawn on land do not develop the special pads, while frogs in fast-flowing streams may have very large pads and extra pads on their chest as well.

Most frogs and toads mate in water, releasing eggs and sperm as they do so. Sometimes many male frogs or toads will try to mate with a single female. When this occurs, the female may be kept underwater for so long that she drowns.

The water in this pond is packed with freshly laid frog spawn. The eggs are protected by jelly until the tiny tadpoles are ready to hatch.

## FOAM NESTS

Some **species** of tree frogs make gigantic, protective foam nests for their eggs by producing **mucus,** which they whip up into a froth with their hind legs. The foam dries and hardens in the sun but remains moist inside so the eggs can develop without drying out. When the tadpoles are about to hatch, the outer foam shell softens and the tadpoles wriggle down into the water below. Many frogs make individual foam nests on leaves or branches and some float their nests on water among weeds and plants.

These African gray tree frogs are making a foam nest for their eggs. Up to 30 frogs may share the nest and lay their eggs in it.

The female African gray tree frog makes her foam nest on dry land. If the nest starts to dry out too much, she visits a nearby pond, soaks up water through her skin, and produces watery urine to moisten the foam.

## LAYING EGGS

Most frogs lay their eggs in masses, but most toads lay them in long strings. Many female toads swim around as they lay their eggs so that these strings become wrapped around plants like long ribbons. The male midwife toad winds the eggs around his legs and carries them until they hatch.

Eggs laid on land avoid the risk of certain **predators,** such as fish, but they do face other dangers, such as egg-eating insects, mold, and drying out. Leaf frogs lay their eggs on leaves overhanging streams, beyond the reach of predators. When they hatch, the tadpoles fall into the water below.

Some African **burrowing** frogs mate and **spawn** in chambers underground near pools of water. When the eggs hatch, the female digs a tunnel to the pool so her tadpoles can escape.

## Hitching a Ride

Arrow-poison frogs lay their eggs on leaves or specially cleared patches of ground. They guard the eggs until they hatch. The tadpoles wriggle onto a parent's back, where they stick with the help of mucus. Then they are carried to water. The dark-colored blobs on this arrow-poison frog's back are tadpoles hitching a ride to a pool.

I DIDN'T KNOW THAT

# CHAPTER 5

# Changing Shape

**Small frogs may be big enough to breed when they are less than a year old, but large frogs such as the American bullfrog cannot breed until they are five or six years old.**

**Most frogs and toads take from two to three months to change from eggs to adults, and some may even spend their first winter as tadpoles.**

**In captivity, toads may live for over twenty years, but few live longer than ten years in the wild.**

**The paradoxical frog lives up to its name (paradoxical means "the opposite of what is expected"). Measuring only 2.5 in. (6.5 cm) long as adults, the tadpoles can be four times longer. They shrink as they grow up!**

## FROM WATER TO AIR

Frogs and toads go through a very dramatic change during their lives. They start life as eggs, hatch into fishlike tadpoles, and gradually change shape, feeding habits, and lifestyle to become adults. This kind of change in body form is called **metamorphosis.**

A tadpole starts life as an **embryo,** a tiny ball of cells inside an egg. The embryo grows and becomes more fishlike. A tiny mouth forms, and the embryo develops feathery **gills** that are on the outside of its body, for absorbing oxygen from the water. Finally, the tadpole hatches from the egg.

This rain frog tadpole is developing into an adult frog inside the egg. Unlike most frogs, it will hatch as a fully formed froglet and not as a tadpole.

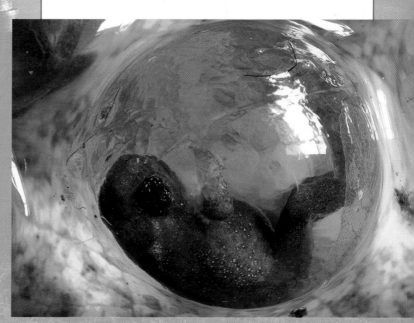

A tadpole's body is **streamlined,** with a rounded head tapering to a narrow tail. The tadpole soon starts to feed on **algae** and underwater plants with its suckerlike mouth. A flap of skin grows over the gills, enclosing them in a chamber to protect them. The tadpole also has a sticky disk under its head to cling to surfaces.

These toad tadpoles are still feeding on underwater plants. Their hind legs are growing, but soon their front legs will appear, too, and their diet will change.

As the tadpole increases in size, its limbs begin to grow and the tail starts to shrink. The tadpole's mouth becomes larger and more froglike. While its mouth is changing, the tadpole cannot eat, but it gets all the nutrients it needs from the tail as it is absorbed into the tadpole's body.

The lungs of the tadpole begin to develop, and the tadpole comes to the water surface from time to time to gulp air. Finally, often before its tail has completely disappeared, it crawls out onto land to start life as an adult frog. It will continue to grow for some time before being able to breed.

Tadpoles face danger from many **predators,** and there is always the risk that their pools will dry up. Some **species** avoid these problems by laying eggs on land. These eggs hatch directly into froglets or toadlets (tiny frogs and toads) no bigger than flies.

The male Darwin's frog of South America protects his young by swallowing the eggs, which hatch inside his **vocal sac.** Up to fifteen tadpoles may grow there, and the vocal sac expands as the tadpoles grow. Only when they have changed into froglets (after about two weeks) does he open his mouth and let them hop out.

## LIFE CYCLE OF A FROG

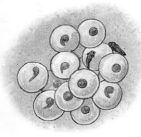

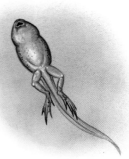

1. The tiny black spots inside these frog eggs are tadpoles. Two have already hatched and are clinging to the jelly that surrounds the eggs.

2. A newly hatched tadpole swims by bending its tail back and forth. Instead of breathing air, it absorbs oxygen from the water through feathery **gills.**

3. Gradually a flap of skin grows over the gills to protect them. The tadpole is now more **streamlined** in shape.

4. After several weeks, the tadpole grows hind legs.

This is a male Darwin's frog. He is giving birth to his offspring through his mouth. The vocal sac in his throat is bulging with more froglets that are ready to hatch.

5. Bulges behind its head show where the front legs are developing.

6. The front legs appear, the mouth gets wider, and the head becomes more froglike.

7. The tadpole is absorbing its tail and developing lungs. It often comes to the water surface to gulp air.

8. The froglet crawls onto land. This leopard froglet is less than 1 in. (2.5 cm) long. It will grow to four times this size as an adult frog.

## LIFE WITH MOTHER

Female **marsupial** frogs from South America are like kangaroos—they carry their babies in a pouch. But this frog's pouch is a pocket of skin on her back with a slit down the middle. During mating, the eggs roll into it. Some **species** of marsupial frog produce more eggs than others. Species with fewer eggs develop into froglets inside the pouch, while species with many eggs carry them only until they hatch, then leave the tadpoles in a puddle or pond to finish growing.

Tiny froglets hatch from a pouch on the back of this marsupial frog. Their mother helps them out by clawing at her pouch with her feet.

Two species of Australian frog called gastric brooding frogs had an odd method of keeping their young safe. A female would hold her tadpoles in her stomach while they developed. She would not digest them like food because her stomach would stop producing gastric (stomach) juices until the froglets were ready to hatch. Then their mother would **regurgitate** them! Sadly, no one has seen a gastric brooding frog since the 1980s, and both known species are believed to be extinct.

The Surinam toad also carries its young around. The male presses the eggs onto the female's back during mating, and her skin then swells up until the eggs are almost hidden. The eggs develop into toadlets inside this safe, protective cushion, escaping about ten weeks later when she sheds her skin.

# Dangerous Relations

American spadefoot toads living in desert **habitats** lay their eggs in temporary pools that can quickly dry up in the heat. To cope with this, they produce two kinds of tadpoles: small ones that are vegetarian, or plant-eating, and larger ones with notched beaks and powerful jaw muscles. The larger tadpoles grow faster and will eat their siblings if food supplies run short. This ensures that at least some of the tadpoles grow big enough to turn into adults before the water disappears entirely. In the fast-drying desert pool below, spadefoot toad tadpoles jostle for space. The larger tadpoles have grown fat by eating their smaller brothers and sisters.

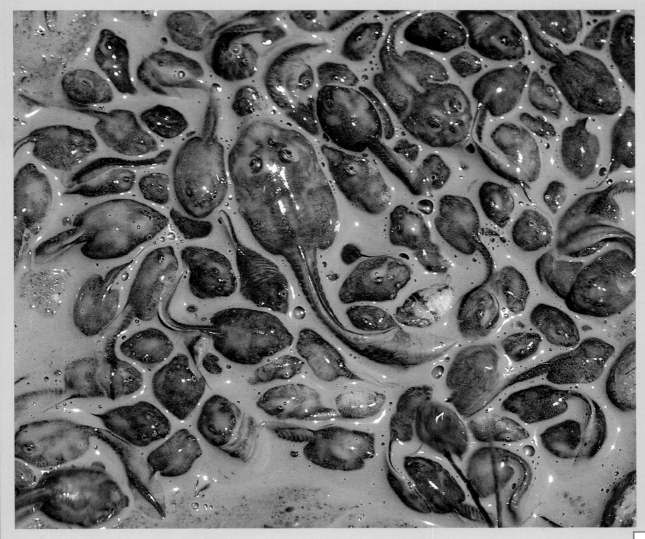

# CHAPTER 6
# Swimming and Jumping

In relation to their body size, small frogs can often jump the farthest. The African sharp-nosed frog, only 2 in. (5.5 cm) long, can jump a distance of over 17 ft (5 m) in a single hop. This is almost 100 times its own body length!

The Italian agile frog is just 3 in. (8 cm) long but can leap more than 3 ft (1 m) high and as far as 6 ft (2 m) forward.

The northern cricket frog moves across water in a series of rapid jumps, using its feet to push off from the water surface. As long as the frog lands with its feet flat on the water and takes off again quickly, it does not sink.

▶ In this frog skeleton, you can see that the bones in the hind legs and feet are long and strong—ideal for kicking out when swimming or leaping. The lower part of the spine, or backbone, is solid like a rod and strong enough to take the force of the jump.

The frog's skeleton is adapted for jumping. Its backbone is short, thick, and rigid. The large hind leg bones have powerful muscles and the ankle bones are long and strong. The hind leg bones, hinged at the knee and ankle joints, act like levers to propel the frog up and forward. As the frog leaps, it holds its short, sturdy front legs tight against its body. The front feet have four toes, and the hind feet have five.

Most toads have shorter legs and fatter bodies than frogs, and prefer to walk rather than jump, but they are able to jump to escape from danger when necessary.

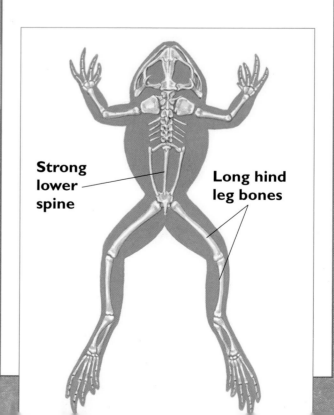

Strong lower spine

Long hind leg bones

When swimming, a frog uses its hind legs to propel itself through the water. Its large, webbed feet push against the water to move it forward. Its front feet are used only to steer or to land. The slippery **mucus** coating on its skin helps it glide through the water. Because the eyes and nostrils are close to the top of its head, the frog can still see and breathe above the water's surface while the rest of its body is hidden underneath.

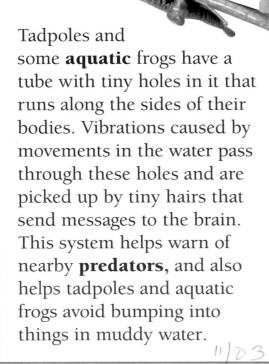

Tadpoles and some **aquatic** frogs have a tube with tiny holes in it that runs along the sides of their bodies. Vibrations caused by movements in the water pass through these holes and are picked up by tiny hairs that send messages to the brain. This system helps warn of nearby **predators**, and also helps tadpoles and aquatic frogs avoid bumping into things in muddy water.

# Flying Frogs

The flying frogs of Southeast Asia and the fringe-limbed tree frog of South America have huge webbed feet. If they need to escape from danger, they leap off a branch and spread their feet like parachutes. This Wallace's flying frog can glide forward for nearly 24 feet (7.3 meters) if it leaps from a height of 18 feet (5.4 meters).

# CHAPTER 7

# Sight and Sound

**Some clawed toads have a special voice box that produces loud clicks underwater—up to 300 clicks per minute.**

**When buried underground, the Puerto Rican white-lipped frog can communicate with other frogs by sending vibrations through the surrounding earth.**

**The Central American coqui, a little frog only 1.4 in. (3.6 cm) long, can make a sound as loud as an ambulance siren.**

**Frogs hear best at low frequencies, below 4,000 Hertz (the measurement of how high or low a sound is). This is about the same pitch as the highest musical note. Humans can hear sounds of up to 20,000 Hertz.**

With their large pupils and jewel-like irises, or colored parts, the eyes of frogs and toads are some of the most beautiful in the animal kingdom. In some **species** the pupils are vertical, like a cat's. In others they are horizontal, or even heart-shaped.

In frogs that are well **camouflaged,** the iris may be the same color as the frog itself, making it difficult for a **predator** to recognize the frog's head.

Although they probably cannot see in color, frogs and toads are especially sensitive to movement, and will snap automatically at any object that moves and might be potential **prey.**

As you might guess from their name, these red-eyed tree frogs have brilliantly colored eyes.

The ears of frogs and toads are just behind their eyes. They do not stick out, but in many species you can see the eardrum clearly. Frogs and toads can hear through the sides of their bodies too, using an area of skin just behind the shoulders that is sensitive to sound. They can also detect vibrations in the ground that might warn of approaching danger.

## What's in a Croak?

A tropical rain forest on a rainy night is alive with frogs' voices. Sound is the ideal way to communicate in the dark or in dense vegetation. Male frogs use different calls to attract mates, warn off rivals, and tell other frogs about the location of breeding ponds. They might also call to surprise enemies. Except when attacked, female frogs rarely call.

Male frogs call with their mouths shut, passing air from the lungs over their vocal cords to make the sound. Many male frogs and toads have one or two **vocal sacs** in the floor of the mouth. These sacs expand like balloons and vibrate to make the sounds louder. This barking tree frog is inflating its vocal sac to make a croak that sounds like a dog's bark.

I DIDN'T KNOW THAT

# CHAPTER 8
# Frog Defenses

**The giant toad can squirt poison from glands near the back of its head to distances of up to 1 ft (30 cm) away. This is far enough to temporarily blind most attackers and gives the toad time to make its escape.**

**The Colorado River toad is so poisonous that its skin can kill a dog. Its flesh, however, is harmless. Raccoons have learned to pull open the toads' bellies and feed on their insides without touching the skin.**

**If threatened, the bright green Darwin's frog will leap into the water and roll onto its back, revealing a belly that resembles a dead leaf. It lies rigid and floats away from danger.**

Adult frogs and toads are **preyed** upon by many types of birds, snakes, weasels, otters, raccoons, and badgers—as well as other frogs and toads. Very small frogs and toads are at risk from large, hungry spiders. Fish, turtles, alligators, and crocodiles also capture frogs and toads underwater. Tadpoles are even more vulnerable to attacks by fish, other frogs, toads, newts, dragonfly larvae, and giant water bugs. They may even be gulped down by a larger tadpoles.

Spot the frog! The camouflage coloring of this Madagascan moss frog blends in remarkably well with the mosses on the branch around it.

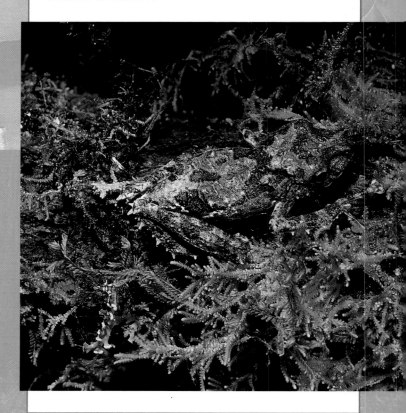

## BLENDING IN

Sometimes a frog's coloring is useful for protection because it provides good **camouflage.**

The nose-horned frog has ridges of skin above its eyes and on its flattened back. With its thin body and brown coloring, it looks just like a dead leaf.

Tree frogs and leaf frogs are often green to blend in well with their background, and frogs that rest on twigs and tree trunks may be gray or have patterns that match the bark. Frogs and toads in sandy places tend to be yellowish, and those in grasslands may have stripes that blend with the grasses. **Species** that live on the forest floor often have the most striking camouflage of all. Sitting still on the ground, some frogs resemble dead leaves and are particularly hard to spot.

Many species of frogs and toads can change color, becoming darker on wet backgrounds and paler as their surroundings dry out.

## WARNING COLORS

Most frogs rely on hiding and camouflage to avoid **predators.** Frogs that depend on poison glands for protection, however, have bright and contrasting colors to advertise that they should not be eaten. A predator that samples one of these frogs quickly learns not to make that mistake again.

In the rain forests of South and Central America, small tree frogs go about their business in broad daylight. Brilliantly colored in

This blue arrow-poison frog makes no attempt to hide from predators. Its brilliant color warns that it is very poisonous.

This fire-bellied toad feels threatened. It has rolled on to its back to display its startling orange-and-red underside and oozes soapy-looking poison from its skin.

bizarre patterns of red, black, orange, yellow, and blue, their bright skins serve as a warning that they are poisonous. This kind of coloring is usually enough to keep potential attackers at a distance.

## SURPRISE!

Often the patterns on a frog's body work to confuse predators. For example, the running frogs of Africa have striped bodies, and their eyes blend right in with the stripes. This makes it difficult for an attacker to find the frog's head.

If threatened, a few frogs that are not particularly poisonous will display splashes of color in hopes of startling a predator. For instance, the fire-bellied toad flips onto its back to reveal a brightly patterned belly. Some tree frogs open their mouths wide, exposing a brilliantly colored tongue. The red-eyed tree frog splays its legs to display yellow and black stripes on the insides of its thighs. As the frog leaps away, the stripes appear then disappear, confusing a predator and giving the frog a few precious seconds to escape.

Several South American frogs have rings of colored skin on their sides that look like huge eyes. If under attack, the frog draws in its legs and puffs itself up so its body resembles the face of a much larger animal. This is a very good defense against snakes, which tend not to attack **prey** they think will prove too big to swallow.

Other frogs and toads drop to the ground and lie rigid as if dead. This foils **predators** that rely on movement to detect their prey.

## FIGHT OR FLIGHT?

Leaping into water is an obvious means of escape from a predator, and so is jumping away. But most toads, with their shorter legs and fatter bodies, are not fast enough to rely on speed for protection. Instead, many will puff themselves up and stand on tiptoe, swaying back and forth to look bigger and more threatening. Other toads simply try to hide from danger. The Goliath frog wedges itself into cracks in riverbeds, and many **burrowing** toads dig their own holes to hide in.

If escape is impossible, putting up a fight may sometimes pay off. A horned toad will scream loudly and bite if threatened, often causing its attacker to hesitate. The hairy frog has sharp claws on its hind feet and can give a predator some deep scratches. Even without claws, larger frogs can deliver powerful kicks with their strong hind legs.

Faced with a snake, this European common toad is making itself look bigger and more fierce by standing up on all four legs.

## Deadly to Touch

The golden arrow-poison frog from Central and South America is just 0.5 inch to 2 inches (1.3 centimeters to 5 centimeters) long. It has such poisonous skin that **native** people simply wipe their arrowheads across its back to make poisoned arrows for hunting. A single frog contains enough poison to kill 20,000 mice, or 100 humans! Interestingly, just one type of snake is not affected by this poison and it is the golden frog's only predator.

# CHAPTER 9
# Frogs in Danger

The Israel painted frog was discovered only a few decades ago near Lake Huleh in Israel. When the lake was drained for agriculture and to reduce the number of mosquitoes in the area, the frog disappeared, too.

More than 30 species of frog and toad have become extinct in the past 35 years or so, and dozens more are endangered or threatened.

In the United States, amphibians with extra limbs, misshapen or missing limbs, and other deformities have been found in 44 states, and involve nearly 60 diffferent species.

All over the world, frogs, toads, and other **amphibians** are in decline. The rate at which frog and toad **species** are disappearing is several hundred times the expected extinction rate for other **vertebrates.**

There are a few reasons why scientists believe that frogs and toads are especially at risk. Their **habitats** (especially the rain forests) are being destroyed by humans for agriculture, raising cattle, timber, and land for building. Also, because chemicals from the surrounding environment can pass through the moist, delicate skins of amphibians, even small amounts of pollution can harm them. A large number of frogs all

These golden toads from the cloud forests of Costa Rica are now extinct. Climate change (a rise in global temperatures) has led to fewer mists forming in their mountain forest habitat. This may have contributed to their disappearance.

over the world have been discovered with severe **deformities.** Many scientists believe these deformities have resulted from the huge quantities of pesticides and fertilizers that wash from farms into ponds and streams.

Frogs and toads are also in danger from the exotic pet trade, and frogs are collected by humans for food in some countries. Many are killed on the roads as they migrate to their breeding ponds each year. In some places, special tunnels have been built under busy roads to allow them to cross safely. People have also set up preserves to protect the breeding sites of certain endangered frogs and toads, such as the natterjack and the European spadefoot.

Sadly, despite such efforts, these fascinating creatures continue to be in danger. It is likely that some species of frog and toad may even become extinct before scientists have had a chance to discover, study, and learn from them.

# Problem Toads

In 1935 the giant toad, **native** to North and South America, was introduced into Australia to control beetles that eat sugar cane crops. This turned out to be a huge mistake. The 62,000 baby toads that were released were not very helpful in controlling the beetles, and they also ate useful insects (including bees, which help plants reproduce), as well as native frogs and other small animals. Because their skins are poisonous, the toads also killed many animals that tried to eat them.

# Glossary

**adaptation**  special feature that helps an organism to survive

**alga**  (more than one are algae) plantlike organism found in water

**ambush**  surprise attack

**amphibian**  ectothermic (cold-blooded) animal that spends part of its life in water and part on land. Amphibians generally have soft, moist skin and lay soft eggs in or very near water.

**anuran**  animal belonging to the scientific order *Anura;* a frog or a toad

**aquatic**  living in fresh water

**burrow**  to dig a hole or tunnel in the ground. A hole or tunnel used by an animal for a home is also called a burrow.

**camouflage**  color, shape, or pattern that disguises an animal by causing it to blend in with its background

**carnivore**  meat-eater

**deformity**  abnormal body shape that an organism is born with

**diurnal**  active mainly during the day

**dormant**  in an inactive state

**ectothermic**  having a body temperature that warms up or cools down along with the outside temperature; cold-blooded

**embryo**  cluster of cells within a fertilized egg that gradually develops into an organism

**estivation**  passing the dry season in a special kind of deep sleep

**evolve**  to develop slowly over time

**excrete**  release wastes to remove them from the body

**gill**  feathery structure on a tadpole's body that absorbs oxygen from water

**habitat**  specific place where an organism lives

**herbivore**  plant-eater

**insulated**  protected from cold with a layer of fat, fur, or feathers

**intestine**  tube inside an animal through which food passes and is either absorbed into the blood or passed out of the body as waste

**marsupial**  mammal that carries its young in a pouch

**metamorphosis**  complete change in form that some animals (like frogs and butterflies) go through to become adults

**molt**  shed skin to reveal a new one underneath

**mucus**  slime containing water and proteins that is produced by most living organisms

**native**  belonging to a particular place

**nocturnal**  active mainly at night

**predator**  animal that hunts other animals for food

**prey**  animal that is hunted by other animals for food

**regurgitate**  bring something back up through the mouth that has been swallowed; vomit

**spawn**  lay eggs in water. The eggs themselves are also called spawn.

**streamlined**  having a smooth shape, making it easy for an animal or object to move through water or air

**species**  group of organisms that share certain features and can breed together to produce offspring that can also breed

**toxic**  poisonous

**vertebrate**  animal with a backbone and skeleton

**vocal sac**  balloon-like structure on the floor of the mouths of many frogs and toads. It expands and vibrates to make their calls louder.

# Further Reading

Arnosky, Jim. *All About Frogs*. New York: Scholastic, 2002.

Deiters, Erika, and Jim Deiters. *Animals of the Rain Forest: Tree Frogs*. Chicago: Raintree, 2001.

Fridell, Ron. *The Search for the Poison-Dart Frogs*. New York: Scholastic, 2001.

Greenaway, Theresa. *Minipets: Tadpoles*. Chicago: Raintree, 1999.

Greenberg, Daniel. *Frogs*. Tarrytown, N.Y.: Benchmark Books, 2000.

Oliver, Clare. *Microhabitats: Life in a Pond*. Chicago: Raintree, 2002.

Parsons, Harry. *The Nature of Frogs: Amphibians with Attitude*. Vancouver: Greystone Books, 2000.

# Index

Numbers in *italics* indicate pictures.